College Planning for Middle School Students

A Quick Guide

College Planning for Middle School Students

A Quick Guide

MYCHAL WYNN

Wynn, Mychal.
College planning for middle school students : a quick guide / Mychal Wynn. -- 1st ed.

p. : ill. ; cm.

"The material contained in this book has been taken from the book, A middle school plan for
students with college bound dreams ... " -- T.p. verso.
Includes bibliographical references and index.
ISBN-13: 978-1-880463-05-5
ISBN-10: 1-880463-05-9

1. Middle school students--United States--Life skills guides. 2. Middle school students--Education--
United States--Handbooks, manuals, etc. 3. Academic achievement--Handbooks, manuals, etc.
4. Universities and colleges--Admission--Handbooks, manuals, etc. 5. Counseling in middle school
education--Handbooks, manuals, etc. I. Title. II. Title: Middle school plan for students with college-
bound dreams.

LB1626 .W963 2007
373.12/0973

Printing 1 2 3 4 5 6

Rising Sun Publishing, Inc.
P.O. Box 70906
Marietta, GA 30007-0906
770.518.0369/800.524.2813
FAX 770.587.0862
E-mail: info@rspublishing.com
Web site: www.rspublishing.com

Printed in the United States of America.

Acknowledgments

I would like to thank those parents, educators, counselors, and mentors who have embraced the strategies outlined in, *A Middle School Plan for Students with College-Bound Dreams*, the text upon which this book is based, and who are working diligently to help more students pursue their college-bound dreams.

Dedication

To my wife, for her patience, understanding, and support; our sons, Mychal-David and Jalani; the thousands of students and parents I meet each year who have college-bound hopes and aspirations; and to those who sacrifice each day on behalf of students and their dreams.

Table of Contents

Mychal Wynn • College Planning for Middle School Students

About the Author

Mychal Wynn was an unlikely college-bound student, having been expelled from Chicago's De La Salle Catholic High School and barely earning enough credits to graduate from Chicago's Du Sable High School. Even more miraculous was his being accepted into Northeastern University, at that time, the largest private university in the United States and the only college to which he applied. Without a mentor to advise him or the benefit of the type of college planning outlined in this book, he had not taken the required courses to be admitted directly from high school into college. He received a *conditional acceptance*—conditional upon his taking and passing classes in Physics and Calculus (courses which were not offered at his high school). As a result of his not having the opportunity to take the necessary classes in high school, his college dreams were deferred as he was required to enroll in Kennedy-King City College of Chicago for one semester in the fall of 1974. While working the night shift at the U.S. Post Office from 10:30 p.m. until 2:30 a.m., he took classes in Physics and Calculus during the day, receiving an 'A' in Physics and a 'B' in Calculus.

In January 1975, he boarded his first airplane as he flew from Chicago, Illinois to Boston, Massachusetts, where he entered into the Northeastern University College of Engineering. In June 1979, Mychal Wynn became his family's first college graduate, receiving his Bachelor of Science degree. This once unlikely college-bound student was a highly-recruited college graduate and has worked for such multinational companies as IBM and the Transamerica Corporation. In 1985, he and his wife, Nina, founded Rising Sun Publishing, where his wife serves as the Publisher and Chief Executive Officer. In 2008, Mr. Wynn established the nonprofit foundation, The Foundation for Ensuring Access and Equity (www. accessandequity.org), whose mission is to ensure that all students have the necessary information, guidance, and support to pursue their college-bound dreams.

Introduction

This book provides a quick guide to the information contained in, *A Middle School Plan for Students with College-Bound Dreams* (Wynn 2005). Please refer to the *book* and *workbook* for the complete set of activities, worksheets, and college-planning resources. *A High School Plan for Students with College-Bound Dreams* (Wynn 2009), provides further activities, planning sheets, and resources for assisting students with the high school portion of their seven-year middle-through-high school plan. Completing this comprehensive set of materials is, *Show Me the Money: A Comprehensive Guide to Scholarships, Financial Aid, and Making the Right College Choice* (Wynn 2015). Equipped with the proper plan, college is within the reach of any student.

Despite the constant influence of peer pressures to conform—to dress like, behave like, and follow the crowd—the uniqueness of our personalities should be as valued as the uniqueness of our signatures. Our personality represents our signature upon this life. Our personality type is unapologetically, unashamedly, and inexplicably who we are. Whether shaped divinely or through the experiences of our childhood, we must recognize who we are and accept or discard it as we continue on our journey toward becoming who we want to be.

— Mychal Wynn

Chapter 1

Understand Who You Are

This chapter will assist you, your parents, your counselor, and perhaps your teacher or mentor to better understand you. The information gathered in this chapter will assist you in developing your *Pre-college Profile® Part I* at the end of the chapter. You will complete the *Pre-college Profile® Part II* at the end of *Chapter 5: Middle—High School Transition.* Whether you are in elementary school, middle school, high school, or already in college, the *Pre-college Profiles®* will assist you in your academic planning, personal development, and career aspirations. While race and gender are the two most obvious things we know about people, there are many more things that we can understand about ourselves and others.

1: know who you are

Taking the time to explore and appreciate the divinely unique person you are will help you to have a positive middle school experience. Understanding who you are can be a pretty complex and scary undertaking. For some people, after a lifetime, they still know very little about who they are, what makes them happy, and what is really important to them in life. For many students, the transition from elementary school to middle school and from middle school to high school can be difficult, disheartening, distressing, or disappointing. One of the major reasons for all of this confusion is that few young people, or older people for that matter, ever come to terms with who they are and how they are different from everyone else.

One of the first steps in understanding and appreciating your divine uniqueness is identifying your personality type. Understanding the uniqueness of your personality can help you better value and appreciate yourself and become more understanding and accepting of others. One of the most important factors to succeeding in school, and experiencing happiness throughout your lifetime, will be the quality of your relationships—the relationships between you and family members, between you and teachers, between you and other students, and, between you and your friends.

Have you ever wondered why you like some people or easily get along with some people while you are always having conflicts with others? Why do you appear to easily understand them while being constantly confused by others? Understanding the uniqueness of your personality can help you to better value and appreciate your divine uniqueness and become more understanding and accepting of others.

Entering a new school year or school setting can be uncomfortable or even nerve-racking. Avoid believing that you have to blend in and be like everyone else. Understanding yourself, together with knowledge of careers which provide the best "fit" for your personality, will influence your future goals and career path. Recognizing and understanding different personality types can help you to get along with classmates today and co-workers in the future. Understanding your own personality can assist you in discovering and pursuing careers for which you are best suited.

Are you an INTP like me or an ESFJ like my wife? Perhaps you are an INFP like our older son or an ESTP like our younger son. After you identify your personality traits, identify the personality traits for your parents, siblings, and friends. Want to know why you continually have conflicts with certain teachers? Complete a personality type profile for each of your teachers and compare it with your own. The relationships between yourself and others can be better understood, and possibly strengthened, through an understanding and appreciation of personality types.

As you go through each of the Personality Type Tables, you may discover that you frequently fall somewhere in the middle. For example, you appear to be an *Extraverted* personality at times and an *Introverted* personality at other times, or you appear to be a *Feeling* personality in some situations and a *Thinking* personality in other situations. As you complete each of the Personality Type Tables, think in terms of your most common traits; few people fall totally on one side of the table or another. Most people, however, can readily identify their dominant traits. It may also be helpful to have a parent or friend complete the tables about you. Compare your results with those of your parents or friends and attempt to discover the "real" you, which may or may not be the person whom you think that you are. Also, keep in mind that we often demonstrate traits at school or in public that may be very different from the personality traits we demonstrate at home or with friends.

Chapter 1: Understand Who You Are

Review the Personality Type Tables on the following pages and circle each statement that best describes you when you are in public situations—those situations when you are around classmates, teammates, or at school. People oftentimes behave differently around close family and friends as opposed to when they are around other students, peers, or strangers. Since you are going to be spending a lot of time in school you should focus on the personality traits that describe how you feel about and behave in school.

[Note: The term _Extravert_ on the pages that follow is commonly referred to as _Extrovert_ in contemporary literature on temperament. The term used here is _Extravert_ as was originally used in the Myers-Briggs Type Indicator.]

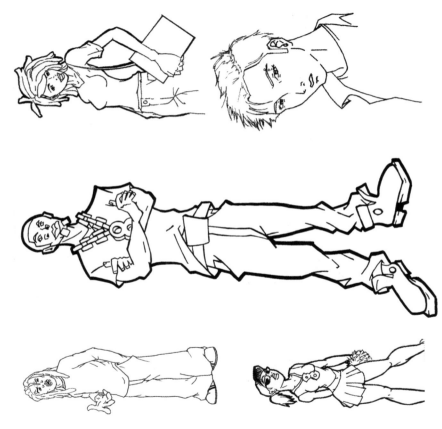

Chapter 1: Understand Who You Are

Personality Types Table I

(E) Extravert (75% of population):

1. I like variety, action, and working with others.

2. I easily meet, get to know, talk to and socialize with others.

3. I enjoy talking while working.

4. I easily communicate my thoughts and ideas in lively, even loud, discussions, where people frequently interrupt others.

5. I frequently talk about things (often unrelated) as soon as they enter my mind even if I occasionally interrupt others.

6. Words that might describe me are: *Sociable, Interacting with others, Outgoing, Talkative, Lots of friends and relationships, Friendly*

(I) Introvert (25% of population):

1. I like quiet, uninterrupted time for focusing and concentrating.

2. I do not easily meet new people and sometimes have trouble remembering names and faces.

3. I prefer to think about my ideas and talk after completing my work.

4. I sometimes avoid sharing my thoughts, ideas, and opinions in large group settings unless it is agreed that everyone has an opportunity to speak.

5. If people interrupt me when I am sharing my thoughts, ideas, and opinions, I tend to stop talking and keep my thoughts to myself.

6. Words that might describe me are: *Protective of my feelings, Territorial, Inwardly Focused, Internal, Serious, Intense, Small circle of friends*

Personality Types Table II

(S) Sensitive (75% of population):

1. I prefer regular assignments and consistency.

2. I prefer working through things step-by-step.

3. I do not like wasting time talking just to be done before starting a project.

4. I am patient with routine details but I can be impatient when details become complicated.

5. I prefer an established way of doing things and I get frustrated by changes.

6. I feel good about what I already know and would prefer not to waste time experimenting with learning new ways of doing things.

7. Words that might describe me are: *Experienced, Realistic, Hard worker, Down-to-earth, Focus on the facts, Practical, Sensible*

(N) Intuitive (25% of population):

1. I like solving new problems.

2. I prefer working on a variety of things.

3. I do not like working on repetitive work and find myself driven by inspiration.

4. I do not like working on repetitive work and find myself driven by inspiration.

5. I am constantly thinking about how to redesign, improve, or change things.

6. I like solving new problems and continually expanding my knowledge.

7. Words that might describe me are: *Multi-tasking, Future focused, Speculate about the possibilities, Inspiration, Ingenious, Imaginative*

Personality Types Table III

(T) Thinking (50% of population):

1. I do not usually show my feelings. I prefer dealing with facts rather than feelings.

2. I prefer to know what you think rather than how you feel.

3. I unintentionally hurt other people's feelings.

4. I like analysis, order, figuring things out and being in charge.

5. I prefer sharing my thoughts and ideas by focusing on the issues instead of on people and feelings.

6. I tend to be analytical, focusing on thoughts and ideas instead of people.

7. Words that might describe me are: *Objective, Principles, Policy, Laws, Firm, Impersonal, Justice, Focus on the problem, Standards, Analysis*

(F) Feeling (50% of population):

1. I am concerned about other people's feelings and may overlook facts to avoid hurting someone's feelings.

2. I prefer to know how people feel rather than what they think.

3. I prefer harmony and avoid discussing controversial issues to avoid conflict.

4. I do not handle personal conflicts well and may be upset long after an argument.

5. I sometimes view constructive criticism as a personal attack.

6. I am sympathetic to other people's feelings.

7. Words that might describe me are: *Subjective, Caring, Humane, Understanding, Sympathetic, Harmonious, Appreciative*

Personality Types Table IV

(J) Judging (50% of population):

1. I work best when I can plan my work and follow my plan.

2. I like to reach closure. I want to complete projects, resolve issues, and move on.

3. I do not take long to make up my mind.

4. I am usually satisfied with my judgment or decision.

5. After completing a project I am ready to move on to another.

6. I do not like interruptions. Interruptions can cause me to lose my train of thought or forget some of the details.

7. Words that might describe me are: *Settled, Decided, Fixed, Plan ahead, Closure, Decision-maker, Planner, Completed, Decisive, Wrap it up, Urgent, Deadline, Get the show on the road*

(P) Perceiving (50% of population):

1. I sometimes do not plan well.

2. I sometimes work on projects without a clear plan and find myself frequently changing my mind.

3. I sometimes leave things incomplete while I reconsider my choices.

4. I sometimes find myself having trouble making decisions; as a result, I often reopen discussions or revisit issues.

5. I occasionally jump from project to project leaving all open and incomplete.

6. I do not mind interruptions.

7. Words that might describe me are: *Pending, Gather more data, Flexible, Don't be in a hurry, Reconsider your decision, Tentative, Something will turn up, Let's wait and see, Are you sure?*

Chapter 1: Understand Who You Are

2: know how you best learn

It is important for you to know how you best learn. Remember, you are going to have to prepare yourself for a race which only you can run. How you best learn is another important step toward success in school and success in life. Your *learning-style* represents the way in which you best process, internalize, understand, and remember new and difficult information.

Everyone has a learning style and everyone has learning-style strengths. It is easier to learn through your learning-style strengths. Learning how you best learn will help you to control your learning at times (for example, at home), and should influence how you are taught at other times; for example, you should share your learning-style needs with your teachers so that they may allow more hands-on activities, if you need those, or use more pictures, if you need those.

3: maximize your learning

Most people have learning-style preferences, but individuals' preferences differ significantly. Learning-styles reflects an individuals' personal reactions to each of 21 elements *when concentrating on new and difficult academic knowledge or skills.* To capitalize on your learning-styles, you need to be aware of your:

- reactions to the immediate classroom environment—background noise such as music and talking versus silence, bright light versus soft lighting, warm versus cool temperatures, and formal (i.e., desk and chair) versus informal (i.e., bed, floor, or bean bag) seating;

- emotional state—motivated, persistent, responsible, and able to exercise control over the learning environment versus a classroom setting that is largely controlled by the teacher with teacher-imposed deadlines, rules, etc.;

Chapter 1: Understand Who You Are

- social preferences—working alone, with friends or classmates, with an adult, or in a variety of ways as opposed to teacher-determined patterns or routines;

- physiological preferences—perceptual strengths (auditory, visual, tactual, or kinesthetic strengths), time-of-day energy levels, intake (snacking while concentrating), or mobility needs.

On average, 30 percent or more of students are unable to remember at least 75 percent of what they either hear or see. They are neither strongly auditory (learn by hearing) nor visual (learn by seeing) learners. Some, particularly elementary and middle school students, remember well when they learn tactually (with their hands) or kinesthetically or experientially (with their bodies—through movement). As your personality type reflects who you uniquely are, your learning style reflects how you uniquely learn. Review the learning-style elements with your parent or teacher. Try to identify as many of your preferences as possible. You may also consider experimenting with different elements to determine which work best for you.

The 21 Learning-style Elements

Review the listing of the 21 learning-style elements and make note of your preferences, like, for example, bright lighting or dim lighting, working on a team or working alone, etc.

Environmental Elements   (circle your preferences)

1. Sound: quiet, background music, noise

2. Light: bright, soft, sunlight, dim

3. Temperature: warm, cold

4. Design: formal (i.e., desk, chair), informal
                   (i.e., bed, floor, or bean bag), colorful

Emotional Elements   (circle your preferences)

5. Motivation: self-motivated, need a push

6. Persistence: will work through problems, need help

7. Responsibility: can follow instructions, need help

8. Structure: need clear rules, prefer to use my own approach

Sociological Elements   (circle your preferences)

9. Self: working alone, working with others

10. Pair: prefer to choose with whom I work, prefer teacher
                  to choose

11. Peers: prefer working alone, prefer working with peers

Chapter 1: Understand Who You Are

Sociological Elements   (circle your preferences)

12. Team: prefer to work on a team, prefer not to work on a team

13. Adult: prefer adult supervision, prefer to work independently without adult supervision

14. Varied: prefer consistent grouping, prefer variety of situations and multiple choices

Physiological Elements   (circle your preferences)

15. Perceptual: auditory, visual, tactual, or kinesthetic lessons

16. Intake: prefer to eat while working, prefer to eat after working

17. Time: morning, afternoon, evening

18. Mobility: prefer to sit, prefer to move around

Psychological Elements   (circle your preferences)

19. Global/Analytic: prefer stories, humor, pictures; prefer step-by-step or fact-by-fact

20. Hemisphericity: prefer logic, prefer creativity

21. Impulsive/Reflective: prefer quick decisions, prefer slow decisions and time to think through the details and possibilities

4: know your best time of day

Have you ever heard someone say, "I am not a morning person?" This statement is true of a lot of people. It is called time-of-day energy levels. Unfortunately, school does not wait for your time-of-day energy level to get in sync with the school schedule. However, if you better understand your time-of-day energy levels—for example, high energy in the morning, and slowing down in the afternoon or just the reverse—you may be able to take a high-energy snack just as you start feeling sluggish. You want to be at your best just before your big test!

Discuss your time-of-day energy levels with your parents. They have had the opportunity to observe you over the course of many years and know if you are an "Energizer Bunny®" in the morning or in the afternoon, if you lose energy after you eat or if your motor shifts into high gear.

Chapter 1: Understand Who You Are

Identifying your low-energy time-of-day may be the moment when you need a candy bar or high-energy snack. Athletes are well aware of their time-of-day energy levels and try to plan their daily workouts accordingly. No need to hit the weights in the afternoon if you are a morning person. I recall watching our older son run the 400 meters. His track coach held a Snickers® candy bar at the end of the race as a motivator during the final 100 meters. Perhaps a Snickers® bar is just the ticket when you find yourself entering your low-energy time-of-day.

5: get a tutor

Tutors, while once thought of as being needed by students who are slow to learn, can be a necessity for students who are not making a connection with their classroom teachers or who are simply having difficulty comprehending or understanding new concepts. As you will soon learn, there are at least eight ways of being smart and no two individuals are smart in exactly the same way. It follows that there are at least eight ways of being weak. One person may effortlessly understand complicated mathematical processes and equations while another will need a tutor. One person may effortlessly compose poetry, write short stories, or write research papers while another will find him or herself in need of help. Keep in mind that when you submit your college application and high school transcript, the admissions officer is not going to care about any mismatch between your learning style and your teachers' teaching styles. He or she is only going to be concerned with your grades! If you need help, do not be embarrassed to ask for it.

6: know your best learning situations

1. Identify the subjects or classes where you appeared to learn the most or did the best and write down as much as you can remember about such things as how the teacher taught, the type of classroom environment,

how students related to each other or worked together, the type and amount of class work and homework, how interesting the subject was, whether or not the teacher told stories or made jokes, and what was fun, challenging, or interesting about the entire classroom experience.

2. Identify the subjects or classes where you received low grades or had difficulty learning. Write down the types of things that caused you difficulty or that you struggled with.

3. Think about the tests on which you have done really well. Reflect on how you studied, how long you studied, what you did to help you to remember the information that was going to be covered on the test, or if the teacher provided a study guide or supplemental materials.

4. Think about the tests where you performed poorly. Reflect on what caused you difficulty or whether or not you prepared for the test in the same way as you did for those tests on which you performed well.

5. Think about when you learn best or do your best work. Reflect on the time of day, whether or not you work with others or work alone, whether or not you are under a time schedule or if you work at your own pace, whether or not the environment is quiet or if there is music, talking, or background noise.

6. Think about the classes or subjects for which you can still remember a lot of what was taught. What was unique about those classes or subjects? Reflect on whether you worked with your hands, created songs, performed experiments, prepared skits, took field trips, listened to guest speakers, received pre-printed notes from the teacher or created your own notes.

7. Make a list of the subjects or activities that you are most interested in and reflect on why you like these subjects or have these areas of interest.

8. Make a list of the subjects or activities that you like the least and reflect on why you do not have an interest in these subjects or activities.

9. If you could design the ideal classroom experience for yourself, what would it be?

10. If you could design the ideal study location at home, where would it be?

11. What is the ideal time of day for your most difficult classes?

7: know how you are smart

Each of us has, or can demonstrate intelligence (be smart) in at least eight ways and there may be many more. Sometimes when a person is really good at a sport like basketball, we may consider him or her as being talented but we are unlikely to view his or her basketball playing ability as being smart. "You got game!" not, "You got brains!" However, when a person masterfully dribbles a basketball or soccer ball, he or she is actually demonstrating highly developed *Bodily/Kinesthetic Intelligence*. This is the part of the human brain that controls body movement and hand-eye coordination.

The person who expertly illustrates comic book characters, cartoons, or puts together color-coordinated stylish outfits has highly developed *Visual/Spatial Intelligence*, not just an eye for fashions or drawing talent. The person who has a highly developed intuition in understanding animals and animal behaviors, camping, hiking, or surviving in the natural environment is highly developed in what is called the *Naturalist Intelligence*. There are many ways to demonstrate intelligence and many types of intelligences. No matter how much you may excel in one subject or struggle in another, you are likely to experience both highly developed and weak areas of intelligence. In some subjects you are likely to appear a genius and in other subjects not very smart at all.

Chapter 1: Understand Who You Are

8: know your strongest intelligences

Review the Multiple Intelligences Tables and place a check next to each statement that describes you. Tally your checks for each intelligence and place your total for each intelligence in the box next to the intelligence.

The more that you learn about yourself, the more you can appreciate the divinely unique person you are and the unique dreams and aspirations you may develop. Take a moment to reflect on what you have learned and ask yourself, "If I could spend four years in college studying what I have a passion for, what would I study?" And, "If I could do what I love to do and get paid to do it, what type of job would I have?" Rather than trying to emulate or imitate someone else, understand who you are, appreciate your uniqueness, and become the best you!

Verbal/Linguistic ▢	Logical/Mathematical ▢
___ I enjoy reading or telling stories	___ I am good at problem-solving in subjects like math and science
___ I enjoy creating stories, poetry, or raps	___ I enjoy doing experiments or figuring out complex problems
___ I am good at writing about my thoughts or ideas	___ I enjoy asking questions and figuring out how things work
___ I am good at talking about my thoughts or ideas	___ I believe that I have a logical mind and I am good at critical thinking
___ I have a good understanding of things when there are written instructions	___ I am good at developing plans
___ I enjoy reading about my hobbies or interests (e.g., books, news articles, magazines)	___ I am good at organizing things into a step-by-step fashion
___ I remember things best when I have a list or by reading about them	___ I am good at gathering data or analyzing information
___ I enjoy word games like Scrabble or word puzzles	___ I enjoy sharing my thoughts and ideas
___ When working in groups or on teams, I enjoy doing the research or writing the presentation	___ I enjoy math, problem-solving, or strategy games
	___ When working in groups or on teams, I enjoy creating charts/graphs or organizing the presentation

Interpersonal	Intrapersonal
___ I get along well with others	___ I am inwardly focused and self-directed
___ I have good friendships	___ I am good at being in touch with my feelings
___ I enjoy talking to or communicating with others	___ I enjoy concentrating on my thoughts
___ I am good at understanding others	___ I do not mind working alone
___ I feel comfortable at parties and large gatherings of people	___ I enjoy meditating and daydreaming
___ I am good at organizing teams	___ I prefer self-directed projects
___ I am good at building relationships	___ I prefer to have my own space and move at my own pace
___ I am good at cooperating or collaborating with others	___ I prefer to gather my thoughts before participating in group discussions
___ I empathize with others and their feelings	___ I tend to have a small group of friends with whom I am really close
___ When working in groups or on teams, I enjoy working with my team members and prefer to reach a consensus on important decisions	___ When working in groups or on teams, I enjoy accepting tasks that I can work on independently

Visual/Spatial		Bodily/Kinesthetic
___ I am good at creating pictures in my mind		___ I am good at sports
___ I am good at drawing		___ I enjoy dancing
___ I enjoy creating models or designing things		___ I am good at building things or working with my hands
___ I have a good imagination		___ I am good at creating new gymnastics, martial arts, or boxing movements
___ I am good at choosing clothing or hair styles		___ I am good at roller skating
___ I prefer to see a picture or a diagram of how something works		___ I enjoy riding bicycles, skiing, or snowboarding
___ I am good at directions or reading maps		___ I have good body coordination
___ I enjoy interior design		___ I find it easy learning new sports or dance moves
___ I have a lot of creative ideas		___ I enjoy putting things together and repairing things
___ When working in groups or on teams I do not mind being responsible for creating the cover design or laying out the presentation		___ When working in groups or on teams I enjoy presenting a demonstration through dance, gymnastics, or other ways in which I can use my body
		___

Musical/Rhythmic	Naturalist
___ I enjoy singing	___ I am good at hiking, camping, fishing, and living in the environment
___ I enjoy playing an instrument	
___ I easily remember tunes, songs, or lyrics	___ I am good at understanding and working with animals
___ I am good at keeping a beat or remembering a melody	___ I enjoy working or being outdoors
	___ I would enjoy survivalist competitions
___ I enjoy writing songs or creating musical compositions	___ I have a good feeling of what is going on around me
___ I am good at picking up sounds	___ I would enjoy living or working on a farm
___ I tend to hum or tap a beat when I am working or thinking	___ I am good at identifying insects or tracking animals
___ I am good at mixing music	
___ I like music playing while I study	___ I notice cloud and rock formations
___ When working in groups or on teams, I enjoy creating theme songs or selecting background music	___ I can feel changes in weather patterns
	___ When working in groups or on teams, I enjoy creating the stage arrangements or building a backdrop

9: know your strengths/weaknesses

This chapter has assisted you in better understanding who you are, how you learn, and how you are smart. After reflecting on what you have learned, identify your strengths and weaknesses as they pertain to your school and schoolwork. Preparing for college will require that you succeed in middle school now and high school later. Middle school is the time in the lives of many young people when they begin to pull away from their parents. There are likely to be many disagreements on the horizon as your parents place a priority on school and schoolwork and you begin to place your priorities on friends and after-school activities.

As previously mentioned, middle school is going to be more difficult than elementary school. You are going to get more homework, take more tests and quizzes, and have far more responsibilities. Identifying your strengths and weaknesses will help you and your parents to identify where you are likely to encounter challenges.

Take time to identify your strengths and weaknesses in such areas as class work, homework, organization, note-taking, test preparation, reading, writing, and within your various subjects, i.e., math, science, social studies, foreign language, etc. Talk to your parents, teacher, counselor, or coach about ways to overcome your weaknesses and to further develop and expand upon your strengths.

10: think about your dreams

I was inspired to write the book, *Follow Your Dreams: Lessons That I Learned in School*, by a middle school student who asked, "Mr. Wynn, why don't you write a book about your life and how you discovered your dreams?" In my book, I share my experiences growing up in poverty and the academic, social, and emotional struggles experienced from elementary through high school. If I had known that my elementary school passions could have become my career, I would have chosen different high school classes, a different college major, and explored a much broader range of colleges and universities.

Part of the process of pursuing your dreams will require that you consider your strengths and weaknesses, and that you set goals. Take a moment to consider the following and then complete the *Pre-college Profile® Part I* on the following page:

- *Academic strengths*
- *Academic weaknesses*
- *Goals for this school year*
- *Life goals*
- *People who support you*
- *Obstacles you will have to overcome*

Chapter 1: Understand Who You Are

Pre-college Profile® Part I

Gender: _____ Ethnicity: _____

Personality Type: _____ Learning Style: _____

Strongest Intelligences: _____ Weakest Intelligences: _____

_____

_____

Strongest Academic Areas: _____ Weakest Academic Areas: _____

_____

_____

_____

High-energy Time-of-Day: _____ Low-energy Time-of-Day: _____

Summarize your best learning situations:

_____

_____

_____

_____

Attach your life goals and your goals for this school year.

Chapter 2

Why College?

The four years of college for the young person just graduating from high school will provide a once-in-a-lifetime opportunity to grow socially, emotionally, and intellectually. The college experience provides an opportunity for exposure to people, information, ideas, debates, and discussions that can shape a young person's life for adulthood, marriage, and parenthood. The earning potential and career opportunities for college graduates can lead a young person into the pursuit of dreams that, as a middle school student, may be unimaginable. However, attending and graduating from college is not simply about getting a better job, entering into a more prestigious career, or earning the right to say that you attended a top-ranked university; it is about the opportunity to learn, to grow, to give back to your university, to make a contribution to your community, and to provide a legacy from which others will be inspired. Your college degree automatically provides substantially greater earning potential and career options than a high school diploma; graduating from a top-ranked university provides you with admittance into a brother/sisterhood of thousands of alumni who are influential in education, politics, business, government, and organizations throughout the United States and the world.

11: what do you know about college?

While some students have parents or other relatives who have graduated from college and have people outside of school whom they can rely on to assist them in developing their plan, other students do not have any family members who have graduated from college and may not have the confidence that they can be the first in their family to earn a college degree.

No matter which student you are, do not allow anyone to discourage you from pursuing your dreams or to convince you that you are not "college material." It is impossible to grasp the full range of options and opportunities that a college education will provide. During the college experience itself you will explore career options and opportunities never previously considered. Your degree will provide you with an opportunity to choose from hundreds of career opportunities from financial management to fashion design, education to entrepreneurship, architecture to archeology, medical technology to marine biology, politics to philosophy, internal medicine to international business, or ambassador to anesthesiologist. A college degree will provide unparalleled opportunity to change career paths, pursue new interests, acquire new jobs, and explore new industries long after graduation. In a word, a college degree is a 'key' that can unlock hundreds of doors and opportunities throughout your entire adult life.

Chapter 2: Why College?

12: test your college knowledge

- What is the difference between an AA and a BA degree?

- What two college admissions exams are accepted for admission into most U.S. colleges and what is the top score on each exam?

- What does Alma mater mean?

- What does Legacy student mean?

- What does FAFSA mean?

- What does Base Year mean?

- What does COA mean?

- What is Need-Based–Need-Blind Admissions?

- What does FAO mean?

- What does your Award Letter outline?

- What does HBCU mean?

- How many colleges make up the Ivy League?

- What students must register with the NCAA Clearinghouse?

- Who is the Valedictorian?

- Who is the Salutatorian?
- What is a viewbook?
- What are the SAT Subject Tests and when should they be taken?
- What is joint enrollment? *(See page 116 for answers)*

13: what do you know about careers?

Not only are these some of the many questions and college admissions terminology that you should know the answers to, but you will need to know the high school graduation requirements and the admissions requirements for your top-choice colleges.

While the four-year college experience can be a once-in-a-lifetime opportunity in itself, college is an important step toward a variety of careers. While your knowledge of the multitude of career opportunities is often limited to the careers of teachers, family members, and jobs available within your local community, there

Chapter 2: Why College?

are many more careers that college will expose you to and prepare you for. For example, have you ever considered a career as an Anthropologist; Cytotechnologist; Actuary; Novelist; or Sommelier? A college education will provide you with hundreds of career options and opportunities.

14: research early college programs

Early College programs are available to students as early as elementary school and offer the opportunity for students to take college-level classes as early as middle school. TIP (Talent Identification Program) at Duke University and the Center for Talented Youth program at Johns Hopkins University are two such programs. Many colleges also offer summer programs for elementary and middle school students in such areas as athletics, visual and performing arts, and math and science. Identify the programs offered by colleges and universities in your area and take advantage of the opportunity to get an early start on college!

Chapter 3

Elementary—Middle School Transition

Most students are both excited and apprehensive about the transition from elementary to middle school. Will I see my old friends? Will I make new friends? Will I like my teachers? Whom will I sit with in the cafeteria? Will I have any conflicts with anyone? The successful transition from elementary to middle school will require that you utilize your elementary school experience as a foundation to build upon. Use the skills that you developed in elementary school to avoid conflicts and to stay focused on your daily responsibilities and schoolwork for a successful middle school transition.

Taking the time to reflect on where you excelled and where you may have faced challenges in elementary school can help prepare you for what is ahead in middle school. All of the subjects taken during elementary school will also be required in middle and high school. Make a plan for coping with subjects you do not like or with which you have had difficulty. Make a plan with your parents to participate in your favorite activities outside of school. You will have many positive experiences during your middle school years; however, you will also encounter conflicts. How you handle these conflicts will impact upon how well you adjust to your middle school experience. If you or your parents need help with your plans, please do not hesitate to ask your school counselor for assistance.

15: choose the right friends

At the beginning of each school year, students are confronted with many types of social decisions from what to wear to what clubs or school activities to join. Perhaps the most difficult decision you will make will involve choosing your friends. Some students have friends from their schools and community. Other students, new to a school or community, are forced to make choices of which groups to identify with, the types of people to socialize with, and subsequently who to become friends with.

16: be a leader

Oftentimes we are influenced by others to do things that we otherwise would not do. Many students violate school policy or become involved in fighting or bullying as a result of the peer pressure of friends or classmates. Peer pressure is not limited to young people but is common in every society with people of every age. Preschool children become part of groups that break toys, elementary school children become part of groups that call other children names, middle school students become part of groups that bully other students, and the examples continue on to adults who become part of groups who commit criminal acts. You must carefully choose who you follow and become a leader for others to follow.

17: have a sense of purpose

As the school year begins, you will be confronted with many decisions and you will receive conflicting advice from friends, classmates, teachers, counselors, your parents, and other family members.

Beginning the school year with a mission, or a purpose, can make all of the difference between a great school year or a miserable one, and between achieving goals or wandering aimlessly without purpose or direction. While the strategies and activities contained within this book will place you on course to pursue your college-bound dreams, they will be of little use unless you have a personal mission to succeed.

Mychal Wynn • College Planning for Middle School Students

18: prepare to succeed

Before you can begin preparing for college or career opportunities tomorrow you must prepare yourself to succeed in middle school today. Preparing for school success requires that you do some work in and outside of school. Speak with your counselor about developing a résumé and career portfolio. At home you can establish a place to store all of your current school information as well as all of the college and financial-aid information gathered over the next several years. Although college for a sixth-grade student is seven years away, before you know it you will be sitting down completing college applications, filling out financial-aid forms, and putting together your college admissions packages.

The information that you begin gathering now will become a part of the college application package that you will complete and submit during your senior year of high school. Depending on the type of college or college program that you apply to, you may be required to submit some or all of the following forms and information:

- admissions application and financial-aid forms
- admissions and financial-aid essays
- high school transcript
- SAT/ACT scores
- academic profile
- personal profile
- résumé
- recommendation letters
- portfolio (if you are an artist, photographer, etc.)
- athletic profile (if you are planning to compete as a college athlete)
- extracurricular, employment, and community service information

The college and scholarship information that you will be researching will not only be important to assisting you in the pursuit of your dreams, but will be valuable to share with relatives, friends, and classmates who are also planning on attending college.

Many families learn that by working with other families to gather the plethora (plethora is one of your SAT words—more about that later) of financial aid and college information that they are able to accomplish much more than by working alone. Consider developing *College Planning* and *Financial-Aid Planning* teams with each group of parents or students concentrating on one area of research and gathering information on college admissions requirements, scholarship opportunities, community service program opportunities, summer programs, SAT/ACT preparation courses, etc.

19: know teacher expectations

Many students discover themselves getting off to a rocky start because they fail to fully understand each of their teachers. Each teacher is likely to have a different personality, different expectations, a different teaching style, and place differing levels of importance on such things as class work, homework, tests, quizzes, and classroom participation. Understanding your teacher can be the difference between a positive or miserable school year and success or failure within his or her classroom.

20: plan for good grades

Understand the grading scale and pay attention to the course syllabus outlining how grades for each of your classes will be computed. A course syllabus usually outlines grades in such areas as:

- Homework

- Quizzes

- Tests

- Mid-term/Final Exams

- Class Work

- Class Participation

- Projects

- Extra Credit

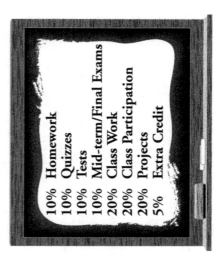

10% Homework
10% Quizzes
10% Tests
10% Mid-term/Final Exams
20% Class Work
20% Class Participation
20% Projects
5% Extra Credit

Develop a plan of how you are going to get the highest possible grade in each of your classes—*Don't leave any points on the table:*

- Do not miss "free" points. If your teacher offers extra credit, these are free points.

- Do not miss the "easy" points. Participate in classroom discussions, do the homework, and turn the homework in on time.

- Identify your weaknesses. If you do not do well on tests, talk to your teacher about ways of better preparing for tests and quizzes. If there is not a good connection between your learning style and the teacher's teaching style, talk to your teacher or a tutor about what you can do to compensate.

If '100' is the highest possible grade, a '99' leaves one point on the table! Each point lost as a result of poor study habits, test preparation, or organizational skills during middle school reveals weaknesses, if left uncorrected, may hurt you in high school. Correcting these weaknesses and developing the proper study and note-taking skills will provide the foundation for a good start in high school and will put you on track for the most challenging classes and on course toward the highest academic achievement.

21: choose activities

Some clubs and activities will allow you to continue to pursue your interests while other activities will allow you to explore new interests. Taking the time to reflect on where you excelled and where you may have faced challenges in elementary school can help to prepare you for what is ahead in middle school. Your counselor or advisor can assist in identifying the middle school programs that will provide further opportunity to explore your interests as well as help you to identify supplemental materials or additional assistance that you may need for those subjects or areas in which you experienced difficulty.

22: avoid discipline problems

Disagreements are inevitable. They may result from someone sitting in your seat on the school bus, bumping into you in the cafeteria, or having a different point of view during a classroom discussion.

Discipline infractions

can disqualify you from participating in clubs, activities, and after-school programs. In some school districts, discipline infractions during middle school will disqualify students from applying to some high schools or high school programs. Ultimately, how you handle disagreements can have a direct impact on where you go to college or whether or not you are even able to go to college.

23: get organized

Many students experience difficulty in the elementary to middle school transition. Students find themselves falling behind academically by the time that the first progress reports are issued and continue to struggle with organization, turning in assignments on time, and effectively preparing for tests and quizzes. Students who are involved in a sport such as football or activity such as cheerleading may also find themselves falling behind in their schoolwork.

After receiving a class schedule or course syllabus:

- Meet with each of your teachers and ask for their advice on how to set up a binder, notebook, or folder in a way which will assist you in being best prepared for their class.

- Make copies of your class schedule and post one in your school locker, one onto your refrigerator at home, one into the glove compartment of your family car, and one into your student planner.

- Place the course syllabus for each class into the front of the appropriate binder. Do not place it into the pocket in the binder, IT WILL GET LOST!

- Create an assignment log and note all of your assignments onto your assignment log. (Note: some students do not find it necessary to maintain an assignment log, they use their student planner to track their grades and assignments.)

- Develop a daily routine of punching holes into all of your important papers and placing them into the rings, behind the appropriate tab, of the appropriate subject-binder.

- Note the due date of the assignment and the date that you turn in each assignment onto your assignment log.

- Place graded assignments behind the appropriate tab (i.e., quiz, test, homework, etc.) and note the grade onto your assignment log.

- Organize yourself in the way that enables you to best track your assignments and grades.

24: develop daily routines

Middle school success like successful athletic competition requires creating a training schedule and pre-competition plan. An athlete competing in basketball, track and field, football, baseball, soccer, or gymnastics does not just show up at the meet, match, or game and expect to win. He or she trains physically and mentally by developing a nutritional plan, training schedule, and engaging in pre-game mental preparation. After receiving your class schedule, you have to take a moment and reflect on your life, the activities that you are involved in, and the amount of time that you have each day to:

- prepare for school,
- travel to school,
- organize your homework and class work,
- travel home from school,
- participate in after-school activities,
- complete your homework, and study.

Chapter 3: Elementary—Middle School Transition

Together with your parents, answer the following questions. Develop the routine that best meets your needs and personality.

1. How much time will you need in the morning to get organized for school?

2. How much time will you need to prepare and eat breakfast?

3. Will you take your lunch to school and if so, how much time will you need to prepare it?

4. Where will you put your binders, books, or backpack in the evening?

5. When will you punch holes in your papers and organize them in the appropriate subject-binder?

6. When will you do your homework?

7. What nights do you have extracurricular activities that may interfere with your homework routine?

8. What days will you go to school early or stay late to meet with teachers or for tutoring?

9. What time do you need to get to bed and how much sleep do you need to be at your best?

10. When will you iron, wash, or lay out your school clothes?

Try your routine for a week and make adjustments as needed to put yourself on the best possible schedule. Post your routine in a convenient location as a daily reminder. Do your best to follow your routine as closely as possible and check off each item as you meet your target time so that you can see how much you are able to remain on track. Remember, this is your plan and this is your future.

25: develop classroom routines

As you consciously organize your before- and after-school routines, you must also develop consistent classroom routines.

For example:

1. Enter the classroom and take out your planner and subject-binder.

2. Make note of the day's homework or announced test/quiz dates in your planner.

3. Remove the current homework or previous day's class work from your subject-binder.

4. Place any handouts, notes, or returned assignments into your subject-binder or folder.

5. Place class notes behind the appropriate tab.

While such a routine may be considered an inconvenience initially, over the course of an entire school year it will become a simplistic and consistent method of keeping your assignments organized and ensuring that you are aware of announced tests and quizzes.

26: take good notes

Taking effective notes is critical to your middle school academic success. Hopefully, you learned how to take good notes in elementary school; however, if you have not developed good note-taking skills, you must bring this to the attention of your teacher, advisor, or counselor. They will be able to make suggestions and review your notes to ensure that you get off to a good start toward academic success.

There is no one-size-fits-all for effective note taking. The purpose of note taking is to record important information that is being taught by your teacher so that you may later review and prepare for tests and quizzes. Each student must learn to take notes in the way that best works for him or her.

There are two important questions to be answered to ensure that you are correctly taking notes:

1. Am I paying attention to and recording the important information?

2. Am I taking notes in a way that best helps me to recall the information for test and quiz preparation?

To answer the first question, you should take notes for a couple of days and then review your notes with your teacher to determine if your teacher feels that you are paying attention to, and making note of, the important information that you will be expected to recall for tests and quizzes.

The answer to the second question requires that you review your notes and determine if they sufficiently jog your memory as to the total scope of the information that was being taught. There are many ways to take notes—from taking shorthand, to drawing pictures, to making mind maps that connect major concepts, to writing short sentences that summarize important topics, terms, or concepts, to using a tape recorder. Whether you use mind maps and lines to connect important concepts, doodle and draw images that help you to recall what the teacher was talking about, or simply write down nearly everything that the teacher says, you must identify the best way for you to make note of the information that is being taught in each of your classes in the way that best helps you to recall what was taught when you review your notes. Experiment with different types of note-taking strategies and review your notes with your teacher, advisor, or counselor to identify the way that is most effective for you.

27: review your work daily

The poor study habits of many college students can be traced back to poor study habits that developed when they were in middle school. Do not make this mistake. Get into the habit of taking out your binders and reviewing your class notes each day after school. A few minutes spent reviewing the class notes from each subject will strengthen the connection between memory pathways in your brain. As these pathways grow stronger, you will experience less difficulty recalling information during tests and quizzes.

The memory pathways that are strengthened from your daily review of your notes will become even stronger if you take the time to draw a picture, compose a rap or poem, or write a paragraph outlining the important concepts covered in each of your classes immediately after reviewing your notes.

28: review your planner

Performing a daily review of your planner will help to ensure that you do not forget to prepare for scheduled tests and quizzes (provided that you wrote down the test/quiz date in your planner when it was announced by your teacher). It will also help to ensure that you are aware of field trips and changes to the normal class schedule, and that class projects are turned in on time.

29: make note of tests/quizzes

It follows that if you review your student planner on a daily basis that you are less likely to forget about scheduled tests and quizzes. Taking the time to review your notes and prepare for tests and quizzes represents a level of maturity that many middle school, high school, or even college students fail to develop. Preparation is key to reaching your personal or academic goals.

30: keep up with homework

All of the work in setting up your binders and your homework tabs will be wasted if you do not take the time to place your completed homework into your binders and behind the appropriate tab. Many students get into the bad habit of placing their homework into the pocket in the front of their binders, into their book, or tossing it into their backpacks. If you develop the habit of immediately placing your homework into the respective subject-binder and behind the homework tab as soon as you complete the homework, you will lose and misplace fewer homework assignments and receive fewer zeroes for missing homework. As a result you will have higher homework grades!

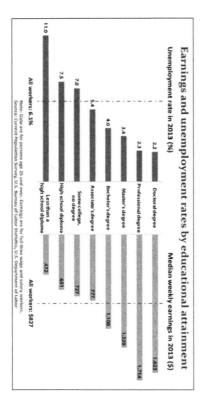

Earnings and unemployment rates by educational attainment

Unemployment rate in 2013 (%)

Median weekly earnings in 2013 ($)

All workers: 6.1%

All workers: $827

Education	Unemployment rate (%)	Median weekly earnings ($)
Less than a high school diploma	11.0	472
High school diploma	7.5	651
Some college, no degree	7.0	727
Associate's degree	5.4	777
Bachelor's degree	4.0	1,108
Master's degree	3.4	1,329
Professional degree	2.3	1,714
Doctoral degree	2.2	1,623

Note: Data are for persons age 25 and over. Earnings are for full-time wage and salary workers.
Source: Current Population Survey, U.S. Bureau of Labor Statistics, U.S. Department of Labor

31: expand your vocabulary

Expanding your vocabulary, developing your grammar, and enhancing your writing skills will be critical to high school success, success on college entrance exams such as the SAT and ACT, and ultimately college success. Developing effective written communication skills and understanding the rules of grammar, i.e., correct placement of commas, semi-colons, capitalization, language and word usage will become essential skills in your high school and college-level work.

Successfully expanding your vocabulary and developing your writing skills requires consistent practice, review, correction of errors, and learning how to avoid common errors. The language and writing skills that you develop in middle school will provide the necessary foundation for success on your high school assignments and on the SAT and ACT exams which you

Chapter 3: Elementary—Middle School Transition

will likely take as a high school sophomore or junior (if you attend an Early College Program you may even take the SAT and ACT during elementary or middle school).

In your Reading, English, or Language Arts subject-binder you should begin developing a vocabulary list of words that will be important to your writing but may not represent the common vocabulary of a typical sixth-, seventh-, or eighth-grade student. You should set a personal goal of identifying one new word during each week of school. This is a modest goal to say the least. A much more aggressive, yet reachable goal, would be to identify one new word each school day.

After identifying a new word:

- write the word onto your vocabulary list;
- write the definition;
- write a sentence using the word; and
- look for an opportunity to use the word in conversation with your friends.

How many of the following words are part of your current vocabulary?

abstract	aesthetic	benevolent	capricious	complacent
conciliatory	devious	diligent	discernible	dogmatic
eccentric	fallacious	indifferent	inquisitive	meticulous
pertinent	plausible	reticent	candid	inevitable
lethargy	morose	novice	obscure	ostentatious
precocious	prevaricate	querulous	quiescent	repose
repudiate	soporific	spontaneous	squander	theoretical
virulent	apathy	disdain	diverse	enigma
futile	gratuitous	hackneyed	incessant	insidious
integrity	jocular	kindle	ludicrous	provocative
reclusive	reverence	scrutinize	superficial	affinity
clairvoyant	emulate	expedite	impetuous	innocuous
mundane	penitent	propensity	regressive	resilient
sedentary	succinct	terse	ubiquitous	vindictive
wanton	zenith	ramification	rapacious	recalcitrant
recrimination	recant	redolent	redundant	refutable
relegate	relinquish	remonstrate	reparation	replenish

reprehensible	requisite	resolute	rigorous	rudimentary
acumen	chicanery	deleterious	epiphany	facetious
homogeneous	incognito	kinetic	loquacious	lugubrious
nihilism	obsequious	paradigm	precipitous	sanguine
unctuous	vacuous	xenophobe	acrimonious	alacrity
conjecture	conspicuous	deviate	disparage	erudite
exonerate	extricate	incorrigible	indolent	judicious
pandemonium	mitigate	ostensible	palpable	rectify
surreptitious	abject	affluence	analogous	arbitrary
cognizant	compulsory	destitute	disseminate	fortuitous
impeccable	impervious	insatiable	oscillate	prerogative
stringent	truncate	unobtrusive	unscrupulous	alchemy
aficionado	ambiance	avatar	bourgeois	chaparral
cognoscente	connoisseur	dilettante	imbroglio	juggernaut
junta	malaise	nirvana	peccadillo	raconteur
vignette	virtuoso	embryonic	entomologist	indefatigable
indigenous	industrious	iridescent	insatiable	insecticide
metamorphosis	larvae	nemesis	nocturnal	pollinate
proboscis	quarantine	subterranean	trepidation	fallible

32: become a critical thinker

Perhaps the greatest challenge confronting a middle school student is to make decisions based on "thinking" rather than "feelings." Middle school students quickly learn that actions driven by feelings or emotions do not require much thought. Actions that are the result of careful and thoughtful deliberation (critical thinking) take longer and require a good deal more work. Taking the time to engage in the critical thinking process when confronted with decisions pertaining to friends, interactions with parents and teachers, and class work can greatly enhance your overall middle school experience.

There are three primary steps involved in the critical thinking process:

- **Investigation:** the process of finding evidence and gathering information. The key to investigation is asking questions and avoiding the inclination to make assumptions.

- **Interpretation:** the process of deciding the facts. After finding evidence, gathering information, and asking questions you must rely upon your thinking skills to process the information that you have gathered in such a way as to formulate opinions, justify positions, recommend solutions, or plan a course of action.

- **Judgment:** the process of reaching conclusions as a result of having engaged in the investigative and interpretative phases. Critically thought out conclusions should meet the test of what is logical or reasonable.

Review the following characteristics of critical versus uncritical thinkers. Place a check next to those that most reflect how you approach problem solving or deal with personal or school-related issues. Consciously work toward developing critical thinking skills and making decisions using the critical thinking process: *investigate, interpret,* and *make a thoughtful judgment.*

Characteristics of Critical Thinkers versus Uncritical Thinkers:

Critical Thinkers ...	Uncritical Thinkers ...
☐ Are honest with themselves, acknowledging what they do not know, recognizing their own errors.	☐ Pretend they know more than they do, ignore their limitations, and assume their views are error-free.
☐ Regard problems and controversial issues as exciting challenges.	☐ Regard problems and controversial issues as nuisances or threats to their egos.
☐ Base judgments on evidence rather than personal preferences, deferring judgment whenever evidence is insufficient. They revise judgments when new evidence reveals error.	☐ Base judgments on first impressions and gut reactions. They are unconcerned about the amount or quality of evidence and cling to their beliefs steadfastly.
☐ Are interested in other people's ideas and are willing to read and listen attentively, even when they tend to disagree with the other person.	☐ Are preoccupied with themselves and their own opinions, and so are unwilling to pay attention to others' views. At the first sign of disagreement, they tend to think, "How can I prove him wrong?"
☐ Practice restraint, controlling their feelings rather than being controlled by them, and thinking before acting.	☐ Tend to follow their feelings and act impulsively.
☐ Engages in short- and long-term planning based on personal goals and available information relating to achieving personal goals.	☐ Engage in actions driven largely by feelings and emotions. Avoid accepting responsibility for personal failures, lack of effective planning, or not having critically examined available information.

Chapter 4

Set Goals

Middle school will present an extraordinary opportunity to make new friends, explore new interests, and experience social, emotional, and academic growth. With all that you will be doing and experiencing, you will need a great deal of maturity to maintain your academic focus; yet this is exactly what you must do. Your academic and intellectual development during your three years of middle school will provide the foundation that will greatly influence your high school and college success.

One way to stay focused on your middle school achievement is to set goals and to track your progress during each of your three years. Remember that this is YOUR plan and you are in control of your own effort.

33: get to know your counselor

Take full advantage of the middle school experience by meeting with your counselor/advisor (or a mentor) to develop a seven-year plan. This plan will include your three years of middle school and your four years of high school. If you are like most middle school students, your plan will undergo many changes and revisions as you experience courses and explore activities. Nevertheless, you must have a plan, you must set goals, and you must work to maintain your focus during your middle and high school years.

Begin by thinking about, discussing, or asking such questions as:

- What are my academic goals during my sixth-, seventh-, and eighth-grade years?

- Would I like to learn to sing or play a musical instrument?

Chapter 4: Set Goals

- Am I interested in dance, drama, or theater?
- Would I like to enter art shows, athletic events, or theatrical performances?
- Would I like to play on a team or join a club?
- Would I like to represent my school in academic competitions?
- Are there other talents, skills, or areas of interest that I would like to develop or pursue while I am in middle school?

The relationship that you develop with your counselor, advisor, or mentor can make the difference in how fully you take advantage of the middle school experience.

1. Take the information that you gathered in Chapter One: *Understand Who You Are* and share it with your counselor, advisor, or mentor.

2. Ask him or her to assist you in identifying opportunities within your school and community to further explore your areas of interest.

3. Ask him or her to assist you in developing your seven-year middle-through-high school plan of academics and extracurricular activities.

34: know your opportunities

While attending school is undoubtedly important and making friends should certainly be part of the middle school experience, middle school offers a wide range of academic, social, athletic, artistic, musical, and special-interest opportunities for personal growth and development that may inspire your future dreams and aspirations. To ensure that you take advantage of the full range of opportunities you must gather information in regard to the complete scope of the programs and activities available at your middle school. This will include clubs, before- and after-school programs, athletics, local, national, and interschool competitions, mentoring/tutorial opportunities, and the full range of extracurricular activities from the Jr. Beta Club to intramural sports.

35: know your academic options

Getting to college will require that you successfully complete middle school. Your three years of middle school coursework should prepare you for a successful high school experience. With a focus on college, you should already be thinking about the classes you will take in high school, the clubs and student organizations in which you will be involved, and the extracurricular activities and volunteer hours to which you will commit. By eleventh grade, what you have done will determine whether or not you have made yourself a competitive candidate for admissions into your first-choice colleges.

Creating a seven-year course schedule will require that you investigate the programs and activities available at the high school that you will be attending. A sixth-grade student certainly does not have to make a commitment to one high school or the other; however, this is the time to begin gathering information, talking to other students, and thinking about which high school you may be interested in attending. Your decision may very well be influenced by the programs or activities offered at the school.

Sit down with your middle and high school counselors to identify the classes necessary to keep you on course toward your dreams and aspirations.

A recent analysis by the U.S. Department of Education indicates that high school students who take algebra, geometry, and other rigorous mathematics courses are more likely to go on to college.

The key to understanding mathematics is taking algebra or courses covering algebraic concepts by the end of the eighth grade. Achievement at that stage gives students an important advantage in taking rigorous high school mathematics and science courses. However, many eighth- and ninth-graders may already be <u>behind</u> in their course selection to get on to the road to college. Some schools do not offer everyone a full selection of challenging courses, or because not all students are prepared for and encouraged to enroll. The results of the recent Third International Mathematics

Chapter 4: Set Goals

and Science Study (TIMSS) confirm that many students enter high school without a solid grounding in mathematics, closing doors very early for further education and better careers.

[U.S. Department of Education: Mathematics Equals Opportunity]

36: explore your interests

Middle school is the time for you to explore your interests, discover your passions, develop your gifts, and identify the subjects and activities that you enjoy. While you can always change your mind, choose different careers, or pursue different interests, you should begin to identify those areas where you have passionate interests versus those areas where you have very little interest. Keep in mind that if you are going to spend four years or more in college that you should be taking classes and engaged in an area where you have a passion to learn or be involved in pursuing a career where you will enjoy the work. Ultimately, the career path that you begin pursuing through your college studies will be one that may last through the majority of your adult life. It is better to move in the direction of an area of study or a career that you love now as opposed to one that you will hate later! Now is the time to begin to explore your interests as you continue to discover who you are and what you enjoy doing.

37: can you earn high school credit?

Some middle school courses can receive high school credit. For example, many school districts award high school credit for two years of a foreign language taken in middle school. The requirements to receive high school credit for classes taken in middle school will vary by school district. Some school districts require a certain grade in the class and require that the class be taken in consecutive years. Other school districts award high school credit for such middle school math classes as Algebra I and Geometry when students fulfill either academic grade requirements or achieve a certain score on an End-of-Course-Test.

38: take your grades seriously

No matter what level of academic achievement you experienced in elementary school, you must now set goals for your middle school grades. Each time that you receive your middle school class schedule, set an academic goal for each class and write down the grade that you would like to achieve next to the class. You must work as hard as you can to pass every class, achieve the grade that you set out to achieve, and perform to the best of your abilities. You will discover that your effort and commitment to perform at your best will provide the foundation for high school success, and later, college success.

39: take your tests seriously

All middle school students are required to take various standardized or End-of-Course tests. School districts use these tests to assess what you are learning and how well you are performing in school. You should take preparation and performance on these mandatory tests seriously. They may influence what type of academic classes you can take, whether you are placed into academically gifted or remedial classes, whether or not you can take higher-level math or science classes, and in some school districts whether or not you are promoted to the next grade!

If you are not a good test taker, then you are going to have to develop better test-taking skills. Your performance on such tests may impact the full range of academic opportunities that you have in your school district. Eventually, colleges are going to evaluate you, in part, based on your performance on standardized tests.

If you were a baseball player and could not hit a curve ball, what would you do? Practice hitting curve balls. If you were a wide receiver and could not catch passes, what would you do? Practice catching passes. If you were a quarterback and could not throw the ball properly, what would you do? Practice throwing the ball. If you experienced difficulty shooting free throws, what would you do? You guessed it. You would practice shooting free throws. If you do not do well on tests, you have to practice and develop better test-taking skills. Failure is not an option!

Taking your tests seriously requires that you review and track all of your test scores. After reviewing your test scores, consciously work to expand your strengths and develop plans to improve upon your weaknesses. If you have low reading scores, read more and spend time with a reading specialist or someone who can help you learn how to read better. If you have low math scores, get a tutor and enroll in more challenging math classes to increase your math knowledge and skill level.

40: get involved in the community

You may already be involved in a church choir, youth program, of other type of faith-based or community program. Consider which programs or activities you may wish to continue throughout middle school, later in high school, and ultimately during college. An important part of your college application will be your community involvement.

41: participate in activities

Many students become involved in organized sports in elementary school. Middle school is a good time to either continue your involvement in organized sports or to become involved in organized sports or to become involved as a means of preparing yourself for high school sports competition. Would you like to compete in

Chapter 4: Set Goals

AAU (Amateur Athletic Union) basketball, track and field, wrestling, gymnastics, soccer, baseball, or martial arts? Are you interested in soccer, lacrosse, swimming, or tennis? Your involvement in organized sports, with good coaching, can prepare you for high school competition, which in turn, prepares you to become a college athlete. Young people who are involved in youth sports programs in elementary and middle school tend to have more success in high school sports. High school coaches think highly of youth development programs that help young people develop their fundamental skills and knowledge of practice routines, game strategy, and the requirements for high school level competition.

If you are considering competing in a sport in high school it would be advisable for you to visit the high school and speak with the coach. Ask the coach what you can do during middle school to prepare yourself.

42: explore your opportunities

In addition to sports, take advantage of the middle school opportunities for involvement in band, orchestra, student government, theater, math, art, science or speech and debate competitions, and interschool scholastic competitions.

During the summers while you are in middle school, explore the opportunities for enrolling in summer programs. There are usually summer programs in the arts, music, math and science. Such programs provide excellent opportunities to explore your interests and prepare for high school success.

If you have already identified areas of interest, e.g., sports, art, science, mathematics, modeling, acting, sailing, etc., enrolling in summer camps, or competing in local and national competitions will provide invaluable opportunities to further develop your talent and gain exposure to a level of competition that will help you to prepare for high school. Talk to other students, teachers, and parents as you gather information about summer camps and programs.

Before- and after-school programs provide further opportunities to explore your interests or expand upon your musical, artistic, athletic, or academic gifts. Participation in such programs may help develop your high school focus or even help you to make your decision as to which high school you will apply to. Current high school graduation requirements include a specified number of community service hours and extracurricular activity participation.

Mychal Wynn • College Planning for Middle School Students

43: be recognized

Talk to your counselors and teachers about the complete scope of awards and recognition that you can earn during your three years of middle school. The available awards will vary from those that you compete for in academic, athletic, artistic, dance, and musical competitions to those where you are recognized for attendance, citizenship, student government, or participation in school and community programs.

Place copies of all of the newspaper articles, honor roll certificates, athletic accomplishments, or other awards that you receive during middle school into your *College Plan* binder or grade-level box (i.e., sixth grade, seventh grade, or eighth grade) as soon as you receive the award. If the award is being given by someone who knows you personally, ask if he or she would write a letter of recommendation and place a copy into your binder.

Chapter 4: Set Goals

44: build relationships

Many middle school students experience some difficulty in the beginning as they discover that middle school teachers are oftentimes more demanding than elementary school teachers. Some students even accuse their teachers of being mean. You must accept the fact that you are going to have more teachers, take more subjects, have more homework, and be expected to be more independent and personally responsible than you experienced in elementary school. However, keep in mind that your teachers are there to help you and it is in your own best interest to develop positive relationships with your teachers. The easiest way to accomplish this is to avoid making assumptions like, "My teacher doesn't like me;" instead, take the time to talk with and get to know your teachers. Share your college aspirations with your teachers and ask them to share some of their college experiences with you. Developing positive relationships with your teachers, counselors, and administrators will allow them to help you navigate your way through middle school, into high school, and ultimately into college.

45: stay out of trouble

To take full advantage of the range of middle school opportunities, you have to take your middle school policies and procedures seriously. Discipline infractions not only disrupt the middle school experience for classmates, interfere with classroom instruction, and contribute negatively to your school's overall school climate and culture, but may cause you to forfeit your opportunity to participate in extracurricular activities, field trips, assemblies, or limit your involvement in before- or after-school programs.

46: assess each year

At the end of the school year you should take time to do an honest assessment of your efforts and how well you did in achieving your goals. Doing so will allow you an opportunity for self-reflection over the summer. While you probably would rather forget about school altogether, you must stay focused on your plan and continue your efforts to recognize your strengths and weaknesses.

Take a moment to reflect on teachers, counselors, tutors, and coaches. Identify those who really helped you as well as those with whom you had challenges. How did their personality, behavior, or teaching style contribute to either a positive or less than positive relationship? How did these individuals affect what you learned in their class or how you performed on their team?

Chapter 5

Middle—High School Transition

A High School Plan for Students with College-Bound Dreams (Wynn 2009), will guide you through developing the high school portion of your 7-year plan. What is important to note here is that few middle school students are thinking about college when they enter middle school and worst yet, few are thinking about college when they enter high school! The question that students should be asking themselves upon entering high school (which they in all probability will not even consider) is, "Four years from now, why would a college want to accept my application into their freshman class? What will be special about me (i.e., 'hook') and what will I be able to contribute to their college community?"

Asking those questions now will help you to begin the process of becoming—becoming a teacher, artist, scholar, musician, scientist, mathematician, entrepreneur, computer programmer, leader, athlete, or web site designer. Taking advantage of your middle school opportunities and exploring a wide range of classes and interests will help to focus and prepare you for your eventual middle-to-high school transition.

47: be an IDMer

The phrase that we use in our home is "IDM" which means "Independent Decision Making." Rather than blindly following the advice of friends, who rarely know more than they do, our sons should be *IDMing*—using their own critical thinking skills to be independent decision makers. We know that their friends use language of which we would not approve, talk about things of which we would not approve, and do things of which we would not approve. By talking to our sons, they know that my wife and I know. As parents, we do not compromise our values or expectations because their friends have different values or expectations.

Are you an independent decision maker or do you tend to follow the crowd? Did your behavior this school year reflect leadership skills or poor decision making based on peer pressure? As you reflect on the school year, were you *IDMing*—using your own critical thinking skills to be an independent decision maker? Were your actions guided by your own sense of right and wrong or did you find yourself getting into unnecessary trouble as a result of poor decisions or negative influence of peers?

Some students will have a smooth transition from middle school to high school, but many others will find the transition particularly difficult. They may find themselves struggling academically, uncomfortable socially, and lost in the sea of faces. Typically, high school represents the largest school setting that entering students have experienced and is not well suited to the personality types of many students.

Chapter 5: Middle—High School Transition

48: identify someone to talk to

All young people are under similar pressure "How do I become the person whom my parents expect me to be and fit in with my friends?" Consider that no matter how much you and your parent(s) disagree about hairstyles, clothes, body piercing, tattoos, music, friends, school, or life itself, you can still maintain a close relationship with your parent(s). While many of your friends may appear to be the most important people in your life, they are in your life for only a short period of time. Years from now you will have moved on, made new friends, and lost touch with most of today's friends; however, your parent(s) will be there for a lifetime. They have a huge role in your college plan and your relationship with them should be one that you can rely upon as you work through your middle school plan. In addition to your parents, you may find the advice of a teacher, counselor, coach, administrator, school safety officer, or mentor helpful in making decisions and coping with the many issues that you are likely to encounter during your middle school years.

49: know what's next

Enjoy your time in school and stay focused on your future. Discover your dreams and pursue life's extraordinary opportunities.

Ideally, you should have begun familiarizing yourself with the four critical areas of your high school plan no later than at the beginning of eighth grade:

- Academics
- Extracurricular Activities
- Personal Qualities
- Intangibles

You should have also begun working through the activities in the high school schedule *workbook* to ensure that your ninth-grade course schedule is consistent with your overall college-bound plan. As you read the high school *book* and work through the activities in the *workbook*, prepare yourself during the summer months between eighth and ninth grade for your high school transition.

As you step through the doors of your high school, do so as the *Captain of Your Ship*, setting your course with your college-bound plan. Despite the stormy seas of high school, stay focused on your dreams, chart your course, and enjoy your high school years as stepping stones toward college and your future career. Complete the *Pre-college Profile® Part I* and *Part II* on the following page. Use your *Pre-college Profile® Part I* and *Part II* to plan your high school schedule and maximize your high school experience.

Pre-college Profile® Part II

Academic Goals: **Personal Development Goals:**

_____   _____
_____   _____
_____   _____

Creative Goals: **Athletic Goals:**

_____   _____
_____   _____
_____   _____

Extracurricular/community service activities in which you are interested:

_____
_____
_____
_____

Top 3 colleges in which you are interested:

_____
_____
_____

3 people who will write you a great recommendation:

_____
_____
_____

Chapter 5: Middle—High School Transition

Chapter 6

A Final Word to Parents

It would be great if, as a parent, you could simply give this book and the *workbook [A Middle School Plan for Students with College-Bound Dreams]* to your child, sit back and watch him or her work through each of the chapters, identify their strengths and weaknesses, plan their course schedule, track their grades and test scores, and remain focused during their three years of middle school. However, such is rarely the case. Some children require your prodding, support, encouragement, and hands-on involvement throughout the entire seven-year period encompassing middle and high school. Some children will even require your active involvement throughout their four years of college.

College planning is a BIG job!

As children undergo the broad range of physical and emotional changes associated with their journey through early adolescence into their teenage years, on more than one occasion parents are likely to question, "Is this my child?" Parents are likely to experience emotions from joy to depression; attitudes from encouraging to unbelievably negative; behaviors from polite to rebellious; and character traits from truthfulness to unconscionable deceit! Perhaps, most perplexing to parents is that psychologists will advise you that this is all normal and to be expected!

Unfortunately, a parent's responsibility for school success during the important middle-through-high school years does not stop at the school door. Nor, is there a particular school year in which your child can be considered, "All grown up" and therefore not require any more attention on your part. Some children will require more monitoring while others will require daily, and in some instances, hourly monitoring. Some children will require little interaction with their teachers while others

95

Chapter 6: A Final Word to Parents

will require that you communicate with their teachers on a frequent, if not daily basis. On more than one occasion, as parents, we have thrown our hands up in frustration after logging on to our school's online grade reporting system to discover that our son had missed countless assignments, failed to turn in homework that we worked with him all weekend to ensure that he had completed, and 'forgot' to inform us of a major class projects.

50: middle schoolers need help

Helping your child successfully navigate his or her way through the middle-through-high school years will require diligence, determination, perseverance and patience on your part driven by your love for your child and your unwavering belief in his or her potential. Enhancing your child's middle school experience and paving the way to his or her academic and social success will require varying degrees of hands-on involvement.

51: make academics a priority

Students today are more likely to be found playing a video game than a musical instrument; watching television than reading a book; and more concerned about how they look than what their grades are. Many households are engaged in a daily battle between parents who want their children to apply themselves toward their schoolwork and children who are intent on learning new video game codes, talking on the telephone, or socializing in Internet chat rooms.

Despite this daily tug-of-war, parents must not waiver in their determination to lead their children if possible or to force them if necessary, to read, write, think, and compute. Some of the strategies that you may consider are:

- Eliminate television between Sunday evening and Thursday evening.

97

Chapter 6: A Final Word to Parents

- Ask teachers for recommended books and develop an at-home library.

- Require your children to read daily.

- Pack up video games during the school year and limit their use to summer and holidays.

- Require your children to write: notes, letters, to-do lists, poetry, short stories—just write.

- Require your children to think: solve brain teasers, math equations, conduct science experiments, plan grocery shopping, compute the household budget, put together a puzzle, build models, etc.

- Connect your child's social opportunities (e.g., telephone calls, movies, parties, etc.) to their academic performance.

- Place report cards and test scores in a conspicuous location (e.g., the refrigerator) so that your entire family is focused on academic achievement and supporting the academic success of everyone in the family.

- Never say anything disparaging about school, education, or educators around your children. If you have a problem, communicate directly with the school or school teacher in question.

Mychal Wynn • College Planning for Middle School Students

52: work together

The importance that you place on education is best communicated by example. Complete forms, activities, and track grades and test scores with your child. Learn to listen to his or her dreams, encourage his or her aspirations, and celebrate his or her effort. Academic achievement is most often the result of effort by your child at school and support by his or her parent(s) at home. The effort of the student who works diligently to raise a grade from 'D' to 'C' is to be celebrated as much as that of the student who raises a grade from 'B' to 'A.' Work with your child to prepare him or her for tests and quizzes, attend his or her recognition programs and extracurricular activities, and continually encourage, support, applaud, and celebrate his or her effort.

Chapter 6: A Final Word to Parents

53: be understanding

Understanding your child's personality, learning style, and identifying his or her intellectual strengths and weaknesses will be as important to you as it will be to your child. If you have more than one child, they are likely to be different from each other. One may be highly organized while one is totally unorganized. One may be introverted while one talks all of the time. One may effortlessly do his or her schoolwork while one finds him or herself frequently struggling. It will be important for you and your children to learn to appreciate and celebrate each other's unique gifts and to work together as a family to assist each other in overcoming or strengthening their weaknesses.

Understanding the uniqueness of each child will also assist greatly in developing an effective system of rewards and consequences. You can be assured that during the middle school and into the high school years that the only way to effectively deal with student apathy and the consistent lack of responsible behavior is to "encourage" them through a system of effective consequences!

54: develop a college focus

It is important for your child to continually hear the college message at home. You must reinforce to him or her that the middle school and high school years are designed to lead him or her into college. His or her work, attitude, and school involvement is all part of a larger plan, their plan, designed to get into and succeed in college. Wearing college T-shirts, decorating your child's room with pennant flags and college posters, visiting college campuses, talking to friends and relatives about their college experiences can all provide an ongoing college-bound focus. Open a savings account, begin gathering scholarship information, and let your child know that pennies saved today can be used to pay college tuition in the future.

Chapter 6: A Final Word to Parents

55: communicate with teachers

A successful transition from elementary to middle school will require that you establish open lines of communication with your child's teachers. Ensuring that your child gets off to a good start in middle school and successfully transitions between the adolescence changes during the sixth-, seventh-, and eighth-grade years will require that you maintain the frequency of home-school communication that is appropriate for your child. Some children require infrequent communication with their teachers while other children require weekly, if not daily, parent-teacher communication.

Some of the important challenges that you may experience are:

- ensuring that your child stays organized
- ensuring that your child brings home the necessary books and materials to complete homework or class projects

- ensuring that your child completes and turns in homework on time

- ensuring that you are aware of when tests and quizzes are being given and that your child adequately prepares

- being aware in a timely manner of your child's classroom participation and completion of class work

- being aware of any behaviors that may be interfering with your child's classroom success

- being aware of the negative impact of peer pressures

Dealing with these types of challenges will require that you:

1. Talk to your child on a daily basis about school, schoolwork, and school activities.

2. Develop effective at-home routines to help your child stay focused on his or her school responsibilities and to help you effectively monitor homework completion and test preparation.

3. Identify the most effective way to communicate with teachers.

Chapter 6: A Final Word to Parents

4. Take a proactive approach to identifying problem areas and meeting with teachers to develop strategies to ensure your child's academic and social success.

Do not be lulled into a false sense of security that the transition from elementary to middle school automatically brings with it maturity and responsibility. These will come eventually, however, you cannot assume that either will come automatically, if at all, during the middle school years.

56: set academic goals

You are likely to find that your children effortlessly establish goals that are important to them, such as:

- reaching new levels on their video games,
- recording certain television programs,
- scheduling trips to the mall, or
- planning to attend movies or concerts.

Mychal Wynn • College Planning for Middle School Students

You are also likely to find that the last thing on your child's mind will be to establish the goals that are necessary for school success, such as:

- recording assignments, test, and quiz announcements in their planner

- completing and turning in their class work and homework consistently and on time

- effectively preparing for tests and quizzes

- putting forth the necessary effort to complete quality class projects

- consistently achieving the highest course grades, qualifying for the Honor Roll, and achieving the highest standardized test scores

It would be ideal if students established and engaged in the diligent pursuit of their own academic goals, however, failing this, parents have to establish goals that are in their child's best interest. Establishing academic and social goals for your child is needed until your child achieves the maturity and responsibility level to independently establish and pursue his or her own goals. While qualifying for the Honor Roll or Principal's List are worthy academic goals, keep in mind that being recognized for academic achievement is a secondary goal—the primary goal is learning. Qualifying for academic honors is a by-product of the effort put forth and the learning itself. Recognition for demonstrating the school's core values or good citizenship is a by-product of demonstrating the character and behavior that brings honor to a student's family and school.

Helping your child to develop personal goals during his or her middle-through-high school years will enable him or her to understand the importance of establishing personal and professional goals well into their young adult lives and beyond.

57: establish a solid foundation

If you use this book, perform the activities, complete the worksheets in the *workbook*, and remain patient, yet persistent, in helping your child to develop the character, study habits, organizational skills, and personal focus on school today and college tomorrow, the transition from middle school into high school will be a successful one for your child and for your family. The strain of the middle school years do not have to be unbearable and the undeniable changes that young people undergo during their middle school years can and should be a largely enjoyable one for the student and his or her family. The middle school years should be filled with experiences that a family can reflect back on in celebration rather than trepidation. However, ensuring an enjoyable and effective learning experience during your child's middle school years will require that you accept your role in guiding him or her along his or her journey.

58: be an involved parent

Be assured that students are less inclined to want their parents involved at school during their middle school years and oftentimes are downright discouraging of any parental involvement during their high school years. However, it is during a student's middle and high school years that they are most in need of active parental involvement as they are being confronted with difficult and confusing decisions associated with their journey through early adolescence and emergence into puberty. While your child is less inclined to want to spend time with you; and less inclined to share the important issues with you; less inclined to discuss these issues of peer pressures and infatuation with others, this is the time when he or she will need to know that you are available and willing to listen.

59: develop an in-home library

Additional resources that you may find helpful in ensuring that your child has a comprehensive seven-year, college-bound plan are:

- *Ten Steps to Helping Your Child Succeed in School [Wynn/Rising Sun Publishing]*

- *College Planning for High School Students: A Quick Guide [Wynn/Rising Sun Publishing]*

- *A Middle School Plan for Students with College-Bound Dreams (book, workbook) [Wynn/Rising Sun Publishing]*

- *A High School Plan for Students with College-Bound Dreams (book, workbook) [Wynn/Rising Sun Publishing]*

- *Show Me the Money: A Comprehensive Guide to Scholarships, Financial Aid, and Making the Right College Choice [Wynn/ Rising Sun Publishing]*

- *Follow Your Dreams: Lessons That I Learned in School [Wynn/ Rising Sun Publishing]*

Chapter 6: A Final Word to Parents

109

60: be patient and encouraging

1. Take time each day to listen to each other.

2. Establish ground rules for engaging in meaningful discussions where both parent and child can openly and calmly share ideas and opinions.

3. Establish high academic, social, and behavioral expectations despite popular trends and changing societal norms.

4. Communicate expectations, identify responsibilities, and establish rewards/consequences.

5. Exercise patience, avoid excuses, and take the time to think before you speak!

References

The content of the book has been taken entirely from, *A Middle School Plan for Students with College-Bound Dreams*. Please refer to the larger text for complete references. Refer to *A Middle School Plan for Students with College-Bound Dreams: Workbook*, for a comprehensive set of activities and worksheets to assist students with developing their middle school plan and tracking their progress.

Wynn, Mychal. (2005). *A Middle School Plan for Students with College-Bound Dreams*. Marietta, GA: Rising Sun Publishing.

Wynn, Mychal. (2007). *A Middle School Plan for Students with College-Bound Dreams*. Marietta, GA: Rising Sun Publishing.

The Foundation for Ensuring Access and Equity conducts college-planning workshops, publishes a college-planning blog, supports high school students through 'College Planning Cohorts[TM]', coordinates book clubs, and provides links to a wide range of college planning and scholarship resources:

www.accessandequity.org

Index

Test Your College Knowledge: Answer Key

AA: *Associate of Arts (2-year degree).* BA: *Bachelor of Arts (4-year degree)*

ACT Top Score: *36.* SAT Top Score: *2400*

Alma mater: *The college that a student graduated from*

Legacy student: *A student whose parents graduated from the college's undergraduate program*

FAFSA: *Free Application for Federal Student Aid*

Base Year: *Tax year for computing student financial-aid*

COA: *Cost of Attendance*

Need-Based-Need-Blind Admissions: *Student financial need is not a factor in the admissions decision*

FAO: *Financial-Aid Officer*

Award Letter: *The amount of financial aid that a student is awarded*

HBCU: *Historically Black Colleges and Universities*

Number of colleges in the Ivy League: *8 (Brown, Columbia, Cornell, Dartmouth, Harvard, Penn, Princeton, and Yale)*

Students planning to compete as a college-athlete in their freshman year must register with the *NCAA Clearinghouse*

Valedictorian: *#1 class ranking.* Salutatorian: *#2 class ranking*

Viewbook: *A book published by colleges highlighting their campus, programs, and student activities*

SAT Subject Tests: *Subject-area tests (e.g., Algebra, Spanish, Chemistry) required by some colleges for admission. It is advisable to take them soon after completing the subject in school.*

Joint enrollment: *Enrollment in both high school and college.*

RISING SUN
PUBLISHING

College Planning for Middle School Students: A Quick Guide
ISBN 978-1880463-05-5
Price: $5.95

To order additional copies, learn about sponsorship opportunities, personalize copies for your school or school district, or to purchase large quantities, contact:

Rising Sun Publishing
P.O. Box 70906
Marietta, GA 30007
Phone: (770) 518-0369
FAX: (770) 587-0862
E-mail: info@rspublishing.com
Order online: www.rspublishing.com